Around Worcester

IN OLD PHOTOGRAPHS

Around Worcester

IN OLD PHOTOGRAPHS

Collected by RAY JONES

Alan Sutton Publishing Limited
Phoenix Mill · Far Thrupp · Stroud
Gloucestershire

First Published 1992

Copyright © Ray Jones 1992

British Library Cataloguing
in Publication Data

Jones, Ray
  Around Worcester in Old Photographs
  I. Title
  942.44

ISBN 0-7509-0158-6

Typeset in 9/10 Sabon
Typesetting and origination by
Alan Sutton Publishing Limited.
Printed in Great Britain by
WBC Print Ltd, Bridgend.

Contents

Hylton Road, Worcester, in flood, captured with style, by W.T. Clutterbuck.

This is mile-little game down here at Worcester.

Introduction and Acknowledgements

I started collecting postcards about four years ago, and have found deltiology to be the most fascinating of hobbies. The postcard not only reveals much information about the past but also stimulates the desire to solve the mysteries it often poses: buildings and scenes you do not recognize; events you cannot recall. The postcard embraces social history, postal history, topography and photography.

I never fail to be amazed by the quality of work produced by our local pioneers of the art of photography. This has prompted me to research into the origins and lives of these early photographers, but.I have yet to collate substantive findings. I rather hope that you might be able to help me in this fascinating research area and would welcome any information you may have.

Please note that the extent to which any one photographer is represented does not necessarily correlate to the amount of work they may have produced. Comparatively few postcards carry the name of the photographer and it is not an easy task to attribute unsigned work. Wilfred Clutterbuck, for example, was evidently a very productive local photographer but I have yet to see a signed example of his work. All the photographers whose work is included in this book are listed at the end of this introduction.

I have been fortunate recently in communicating with the descendants of Percy Parsons and they have provided me with a wealth of information which I hope will be published in the future.

The photographs I have chosen for this compilation illustrate aspects of Worcester and the surrounding area that have perhaps not been fully covered in previous works. The emphasis has been placed on rural and urban change and I will leave it largely up to you to decide how beneficial these changes have been. Undoubtedly these changes have been most rapid and extensive in and near Worcester and some of the local landscape has changed beyond recognition. In the more isolated villages and hamlets change has not been so intrusive and they remain superficially the same as they were nearly a century ago.

I would like to thank all those people who have encouraged me in the pursuit of my hobby and these include Mike Grundy of the *Worcester Evening News*, George Sawyer, Chris Garner, John Brettell, Brian Standish and Ron Shuard. I also acknowledge the excellent research done by Bill Gwilliam, Mike Hallett and the Haynes brothers, which has made the task of compiling this book that much easier.

Special thanks are due to Keith Boulton of Broadheath for the use of his precious photographs, and to my wife for her patience in the face of mounds of paperwork.

(Please note that in most cases dates are only approximate):

EB	Edward and Frank Baldwin – 12 The Tything, Worcester (1938–53).
HB	H. Bevan – Shelsley Beauchamp (?).
AC	George Colwell – Greenhill Villa, London Road, Worcester (1908–24).
WC	W.H. Cox – Wichenford (1938–40).
WTC	Wilfred Thomas Clutterbuck – 29 Bozward Street, St John's, Worcester (1904–10).
FD	Frederick Downing – 21 Ombersley Road, Worcester (1908–9).
	– 16 Edgar Street, Worcester (1910–15).
WD	William W. Dowty – 8 Broad Street, Worcester (1916–56).
JF	J. Parkes Foy – 57 The Tything, Worcester (1924–40).
MF	Max Fischer – 10 Barbourne Road, Worcester and 33 Lowesmoor, Worcester (1908–17).
GH	Geoffrey Hopcraft – 57 The Tything, Worcester (1950–89).
WH	Walter W. Harris – 101 High Street, Worcester (1904–24).
HI	Henry Iliffe – 38 High Street, Worcester (1910).
	– 57 The Tything, Worcester (1912–19).
JP	Jane Pitt and Son – 2 Park Avenue, Worcester (1908–12).
PP	Percy Parsons – 20–1 St Nicholas Street, Worcester (1888–1905).
	– 4 College Street, Worcester (1908–12).
	– 13 Summer Street, Worcester (1914–31).
BS	Thomas Bennett & Son – 8 Broad Street, Worcester (1879–1916).
WW	William Wilkins – 74 Northwick Road, Worcester (1917–24).
MX	Maxton – Kempsey (1913–17).

Worcester

This selection of photographs covers both the familiar and the forgotten. Many superb buildings and streets have been lost in the last century, but to what extent was this necessary? While change is inevitable should not more effort have been made to preserve the irreplaceable? Certainly many mistakes were made in the past, and the chance to make Worcester another York was lost because of the fervent desire to replace the old with the new. The recent development schemes of Reindeer Court and CrownGate are encouraging in that they have preserved the best of the old while still stimulating the economy of the city. On the fringes of the city the conflict between town and country continues, as close lying villages struggle to retain their identity, but it is hoped that the green belt policy will ensure the survival of treasured surroundings. Worcester remains a city of great character despite its losses and will always be a popular destination for tourists.

Worcester Cathedral viewed from the gardens of the Deanery. The card was posted in 1928. (WH)

Vergers outside the Cathedral, *c.* 1910. (WH)

The bread dole in 1909. (WH)

Volunteer workers pose in front of a captured German biplane and tank, which are proudly displayed in front of the Cathedral. (WH)

The unveiling of the South African War Memorial on 23 September 1908. (BS)

THE COLLEGE PRIVATE COMMERCIAL HOTEL & RESTAURANT, ═══════════════WORCESTER.═══════

Delightfully situated opposite the Cathedral.   Terms on Application.   MRS. M. PARSONS, Proprietress.

An advertisement card published by Burrow of Cheltenham and posted in 1907. The proprietress of The College is Mrs Maud Parsons, the wife of Percy Parsons – the early local photographer.

Another advertisement card – posted on 9 March 1917. Reg writes: 'Arrived Worcester one o'clock, we have now got a three mile walk to the barracks – deep snow here.'

College Street and Friar Street, *c.* 1904. Published by Burrow.

College Street in the roaring twenties. The electric tram is on the London Road route and is advertising the Scala Cinema.

Sidbury in July 1939. The horse-drawn delivery cart above belongs to the well-known Claptons bakery, situated at No. 31 Sidbury. The cart is actually parked outside the White Hart Inn, which can also be seen in the background of the previous photograph. Pictured left is the Angel Commercial Hotel at No. 36 Sidbury, which has since been demolished.

This building, similar in style to 'Ye Old Deanery', was situated at No. 21 Lich Street. This street was a victim of the Lichgate development scheme of the 1960s. (WH)

Lich Gate in the 1950s, looking towards Lich Street. Bodies used to pass through here before burial in a churchyard situated north-east of the Cathedral. Lich Gate may have been the only surviving one of its type in Europe and its demolition in 1962 should surely have been avoided.

Copenhagen Street, *c.* 1910. In the foreground is No. 9 The Court, known as Trafalgar Place, which possessed a magnificent ornately carved barge-board. In the background are the Model Dwelling Houses of St Albans Square. All these buildings have now been demolished. (WH)

Birdport, *c.* 1910. The building on the left is the Glovers Arms at No. 19 Powick Lane, which was run by Mrs Mary Ann Hale. Powick Lane was situated just to the north of the Countess of Huntingdon's chapel, which is now admirably preserved within the CrownGate development. (WH)

St Andrews church, *c*. 1910. This view is from Hounds Lane, which was to the north-west of the church. (WH)

Broad Street, *c.* 1937. Berrows' *Worcester Journal* offices are on the right-hand side.

Angel Place before the Centrovincial and CrownGate developments.

Early advertising card depicting the New Theatre Royal, Angel Street. It was published by Burrow around 1912. This fine building was lost to Worcester in 1962, and a super-market now occupies the site.

Irene Carrington appeared in *A Woman's Past* at the New Theatre Royal in August 1906.

The Knights performed in January 1917.

Worcester Grammar School for Girls, *c*. 1907. Known as Northwall House, this building is situated in The Butts and is in a sad state of disrepair.

The Trinity House pictured before its removal in 1891. The building was moved because it was decided to extend Trinity Street through to St Nicholas Street. There was a possibility that it would be demolished, so we must be grateful for the engineering skills of the local firm of Bromage and Evans who moved the building about 30 ft to its present position. (WH)

The Reindeer Court development is named after this hotel – pictured right from Mealcheapen Street, and below from the courtyard. Both postcards published by Burrow around 1905.

Pitchcroft has always been a popular venue for fêtes over the years. Here are two fine photographs illustrating the work of Percy Parsons (above) and George Colwell (below). Colwell's photograph depicts 'Dr Cook at the North Pole' on a Lifeboat Saturday in the summer of 1909.

Pitchcroft was the venue for the Unionist fête in 1913. (MF)

Pitchcroft was also the scene of the Three Counties Show in 1924. Unfortunately the River Severn flooded and ruined the event. (JF)

Worcester Bridge, *c.* 1904. The boat featured is the *Perseverance*, which operated between 1868 and 1904. She was then converted into a boathouse before being broken up in the 1950s.

The electricity works dominate this view of the River Severn. The works had been extended in 1942 and this addition with its three tall chimneys resulted in the '*Queen Mary*' look. The works were closed down in 1975 and largely demolished in 1979.

Two views of the popular steamer trips, photographed by the Empire Studio in the early 1900s. These photographs were sold to the happy trippers. The *Belle* was brought to Worcester by Harry Everton in 1896, after a voyage around the coast from London and up the River Severn.

Diglis viewed from the Cathedral, *c.* 1950.

Diglis House, *c.* 1910. Liquid refreshment was provided by Andrew Carpenter.

Worcestershire County Cricket ground, New Road, *c.* 1905. The club moved here from Boughton in 1896.

Hats appear to be very popular in this New Road scene of the 1930s.

Two views of Cripplegate Park in the 1930s. The photograph above features a section of the old Worcester Bridge which was removed in 1847 during extension work. Alas, it has since been severely vandalized.

Pitmaston is now a well-known local school. George Fletcher Twemlow was the owner in 1908. (WH)

Bromyard Road, *c.* 1910. This is no longer such a quiet thoroughfare!

GARAGE - Open Day and Night.

THE STAR COUNTY AND FAMILY HOTEL, WORCESTER.
G. E. SPURR. Proprietor.
Telephone No. 203.
Telegrams: "Star Hotel, Worcester."

The Star Hotel was quick to cater for the needs of the new motoring public. In an advertisement of 1908 The Star also boasted of 'electric light throughout, ladies' drawing-room, billiard and smoking-rooms, and perfect sanitation'. Among its famous clientele were Sir Ernest Shackleton, Bonar Law, Stanley Baldwin and Vesta Tilley.

HOTEL LOUNGE.

The STAR County & Family Hotel,
WORCESTER, England.
GARAGE · OPEN DAY AND NIGHT.
TELEPHONE NO. 203 (2 LINES).
TELEGRAMS: STAR HOTEL, WORCESTER.
G. E. SPURR, Proprietor.

Sansome Walk photographed from a high vantage point – probably the railway bridge. The card was posted in 1918.

Foregate Street, *c.* 1914.

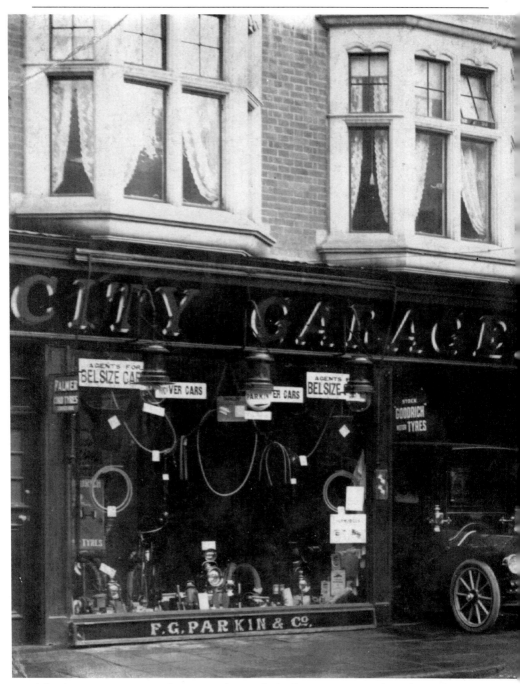

The City Garage was run by F.G. Parkin in the early 1900s. Situated in The Tything, this garage still survives today under the long ownership of the Wild family.

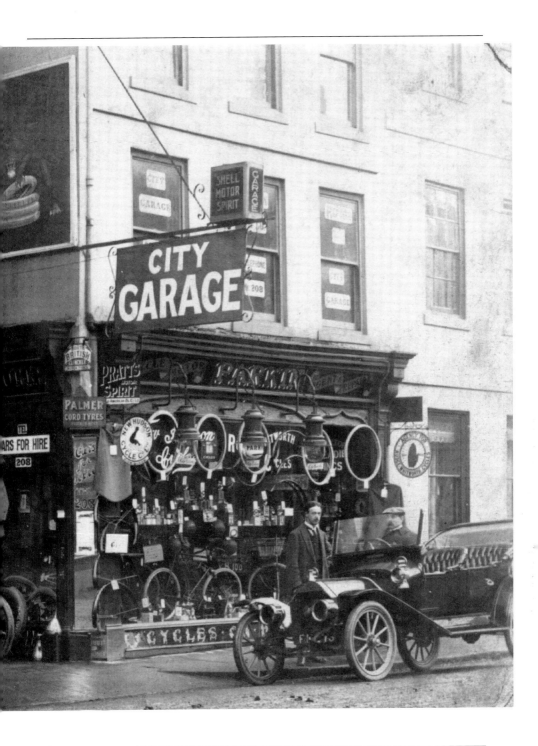

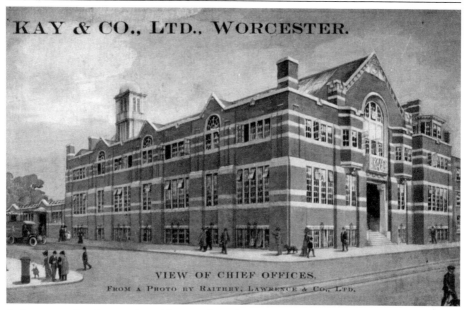

A fine example of an early trading card used in mail order correspondence by Kay and Co. Ltd.

St Georges Square, c. 1910. There has been a church here since 1830, but the current church was consecrated in 1895.

The old water tower was situated towards the river end of Tower Road. Water was pumped from the river into a tank at the top of the tower, and from there to a central reservoir close to the site of Trinity House. Unfortunately the tower was demolished in the late 1950s. (WH)

Tower Road, *c.* 1910. The view is little changed today, although motor vehicles could not gain access via Lavender Road at this time. (JP)

Barbourne College, *c.* 1904. This was a boarding school for boys and has long since been demolished. The grounds now form part of Gheluvelt Park.

Two familiar scenes of Gheluvelt Park in the 1930s.

24 WAR MEMORIAL COTTAGES,
CHELUVELT PARK, WORCESTER.

The New Inn, Ombersley Road, c. 1905. Apart from housing in Whinfield Road this was largely a rural setting.

Perdiswell Hall, c. 1910. Built in the 1780s, the main building was demolished in 1956 after being gutted by fire. The remaining stables have been used by the city parks department for some years, while part of the former entrance gates still stands on the Droitwich Road opposite Checketts Lane.

Astwood Road, *c.* 1925. This was on a tramway route from The Cross which terminated at Astwood Cemetery!

Tunnel Hill, *c.* 1912. Many of these homes were occupied by railway workers.

Terrace Walk, *c.* 1912. Occupants included railway workers, commercial travellers and a glove cutter. (MF)

Shrub Hill Road in the 1940s. On the left is Holy Trinity church which was demolished in 1969. At one time there were many public houses between The Cross and Shrub Hill station and three feature in this photograph: the Prince of Wales, the Railway Arms, and the Great Western Hotel. The 'Vinegar Line' operated until the 1960s.

Wylds Lane in the 1920s. The shop on the corner of Compton Road was a confectioners, while on the extreme right the premises of J. and N. Nadin – the local coal merchants – are just discernible.

Battenhall Mount, c. 1910. This was once the home of the Allsop brewing family and now forms part of St Mary's Convent School. The great-grandson of Percy Parsons – Christopher Garner – is now deputy headteacher at this school. (PP)

Battenhall College, *c.* 1910. This was a private girls' school run by Miss Alice Woodward. It later became a boarding-house for the Kings School and has now been converted into flats. (PP)

Berwicks Bridge was a charming humpback bridge that used to span Duck Brook near Diglis. Sadly it was pulled down in the 1960s to make way for an access road to new housing developments. (WH)

Bury's Garage, c. 1940. This garage was situated on the Bath Road between Wheatfield Avenue and the Ketch Hotel.

Perry Wood, *c*. 1910. This idyllic scene was transformed by the opening of a new Metal Box factory in May 1931.

The Cottage, Upper Wick, in the 1930s. This postcard was published for J.H. Chalke who ran the Rushwick Post Office.

Lovers' Bridge, Boughton, *c.* 1924.

Worcester's first electric tramcar in February 1904. On 31 May 1928 all the electric tram-cars were withdrawn from service and were replaced by motor omnibuses on all city routes.

Worcester's motor omnibus fleet in 1912. These omnibuses worked primarily between Worcester and local villages such as Kempsey, Ombersley, Hallow, Powick and Callow End. (AC)

The world famous carriage manufacturers of McNaught and Co. were situated at Nos 9–10 The Tything. This trading card was posted in 1906. The premises of Kay and Co. now stand on the site of the huge McNaught workshops where more than 100 highly skilled men were employed. One small reminder of the company remains – McNaught Place, a short cul-de-sac off Sansome Walk.

An early motor omnibus owned by Midland Red, who reached an agreement with Worcester Corporation in 1928 to operate all bus services in the city.

Foregate Street station pictured on 15 July 1919.

Shrub Hill station, *c.* 1915. The glazed roof was removed during the 1930s.

The Shirehall was the scene of many military gatherings in past years. The above scene was captured on film by Max Fischer, while the Territorials below were photographed by W.W. Dowty in 1914.

ORNAMENTAL HEART-SHAPED Floral Emblem

ARTISTIC AND APPROPRIATE DESIGN.

Price 7/6, 10/6, 15/-, 21/- and upwards.

Fresh Cut Flowers and Floral Designs
OF EVERY DESCRIPTION AT SHORTEST NOTICE.

W. B. ROWE & SON, Nurserymen and Seedsmen, **WORCESTER.**

The nurseries of W.B. Rowe and Son were situated on the Droitwich Road close to the junction with Bilford Road. Trading was carried out from No. 65 Broad Street. This advertisement card was posted in 1906.

GASCOYNE'S Selected
BIG SEEDS
give BIG CROPS

Gascoyne, Son and Buckland traded in clover and grasses from No. 21 Sansome Street.

The Dyson Perrins Museum in Severn Street, c. 1906. Now enlarged, this museum houses the finest collection of Royal Worcester porcelain in the world.

The impressive façade of the Royal Worcester porcelain showrooms, c. 1938.

St Peter's School in Severn Street has now become part of the Dyson Perrins Museum. Among those pictured here in 1932 are the following. Back row, first from left: Mr Thomasson (headmaster). Second from left: Fong Keng (who lived at the Chinese laundry in Friar Street). Fourth row, sixth from left: Bill Thomas (who informs me that several of his fellow pupils were killed in the Second World War).

The Lansdowne public house and regulars, *c.* 1920.

Members of the 1924 carnival float entered by the Worcester Oddfellows. Three sisters are among the group: Vernal, Anne ('Cis') and Daisy Corbett. Vernal and 'Cis' are on the extreme left and right of the second row from the back, both dressed as 'Red Indians'. Daisy is kneeling on the right of the front row in shorts, black stockings and a very large hat. (AC)

The workers of Stoke Bros., who were based at Laugherne Road, *c.* 1908.

Worcester Corporation workmen, *c.* 1910. They are probably posing outside the stores, situated at No. 20 The Butts.

Worcester City football team pictured in 1907. Back row, left to right: T. Swinbourne.
T. Turner. J. Fletcher. Second row: T. Tudor, H. King, J. Mason, S. Legge, T. Perkins.
Front row: A. Price, J. Gould, J. Phipps.

The Worcestershire Senior Cup. (FD)

Vesta Tilley was a highly popular music hall artiste for over 40 years. She was born in the Blockhouse area on 13 May 1864 and named Matilda Alice Victoria Powles. She performed all over the country but returned to Worcester several times – at first to appear at the Alhambra music hall and the New Concert Hall (now Vesta Tilley House), and then to top the bill at the Public Hall in 1913. She died in London at the age of 88, as Lady de Frece.

The 'Starlight Follies' in action around 1940, at the Starlight Dancing Academy. This was above Croad's flower shop in the High Street where the Russell and Dorrell store now stands. Left to right: Mary Harman (now Mrs Inight), Betty Burbidge (now Mrs High), Barbara Drew (now Mrs Lomas and living in New Zealand), Rosemary Allbutt (now Mrs Blackburn), Elsie Andrews, Dorothy Vobe. (EB)

The Eltex skittles team in the early 1950s. Back row, left to right: Eugene Dinsdale (my uncle), L. Goodyear, Les Hughes, J. Roach, George Elt (of Eltex), Gerald Rose, Bill Dovey, Horace Knibb, Jack Cotterill, -?-. Front row: -?-, -?-, George Jones (my father), 'Ginger' Goodyear, ? Stevens.

We leave Worcester for the countryside with this superb study of proud boat owners on the River Severn, *c.* 1910. (AC)

Claines, Fernhill Heath and Hindlip

Most of the ancient parish of Claines has now been lost to the City of Worcester, and Claines church now sits in a small rural oasis surrounded by either urban sprawl or busy major roads. Fernhill Heath lies astride the bustling A38 between Worcester and Droitwich and serves both centres as a large dormitory village. This is a far cry from the *Kelly's Directory* entry of 1924 which describes Fernhill Heath as 'a hamlet with a station on the Great Western Railway; the kennels of the Worcestershire Foxhounds are here' (as they still are today). Hindlip is an historic place, having connections with the Habington family of 'Gunpowder Plot' fame. Hindlip is now best known as housing the West Mercia Constabulary Headquarters.

Claines church in wintry splendour, *c.* 1910. Elgar visited the churchyard as a boy to study musical scores near the graves of his maternal grandparents. (WH)

The Mug House is situated within Claines churchyard. Albert Beck was mine host for the religious drinkers!

A motley collection of regulars outside the Halfway House, Fernhill Heath, c. 1911. Harry Wild was the licensee.

The Worcestershire Hunt outside the White Hart Inn, Fernhill Heath, photographed around 1908 when the licensee was John Brickell. (PP)

The main road through Fernhill Heath, *c.* 1927. In the background is the Halfway House. (PP)

Hindlip Hall, *c.* 1910. Then the home of Lord Hindlip, it is now occupied by 'the boys in blue'! (WH)

Hindlip Court and farm, *c.* 1922. This postcard was published for L.B. Barnett, who ran the post office in Fernhill Heath.

Warndon, Trotshill and Spetchley

The parish of Warndon (which included Trotshill) had a population of only 141 in 1901. This was primarily a farming area, with only a blacksmith and a wheel-cutter to serve the needs of the local community. In recent years, however, Worcester's urban expansion has replaced the traditional farms with vast new housing estates. Trotshill Lane is no longer a scenic back road out of Worcester, but if you search carefully you will find that its rustic charm still persists in the form of a rural cul-de-sac. Spetchley is a small parish, which was dominated for centuries by the Berkeley family – who continue to reside at Spetchley Court. Although Worcester grows ever nearer, the scattered dwellings of Spetchley remain well preserved and worthy of closer inspection.

The Old Parsonage Farm, c. 1906. This was glebe cottages in the early 1900s and more recently the home of Sir Peter Walker. (WH)

Two views of The Artist's Cottage at Trotshill, *c.* 1906. This was so called because several local artists were reputed to have painted it, including the renowned B.W. Leader. This cottage was badly damaged by a fire in the thatch around 1937, but was fortunately refurbished in 1940. In recent times the cottage has been extended and is now called Mabs Cottage. This reflects its earlier days as Mabs Tenement in the 1650s. (WH)

An old grain store at Trotshill Farm, *c*. 1906. This still sits on its staddlestones today and is known locally as 'the old apple store'. (WH)

A Trotshill cottage in rural splendour, *c*. 1906. No wonder that Trotshill was once described as 'an ideal of a forest hamlet of the days of Robin Hood'. Unfortunately, few of the original thatched cottages now survive. (WH)

Two views of the main road through Spetchley, *c.* 1906. Back in the 1850s this had been the main route from Worcester to its railway station, to the east of Spetchley Park. The journey was undertaken by means of a ramshackle one-horse bus, or if the weather was bad by 'Shank's pony' along muddy roads! (WH)

Looking towards Worcester from Spetchley church, *c.* 1906. This small church contains interesting monuments of the Berkeley family.

Spetchley Farm, *c.* 1906. This farm belonged to the Spetchley estate. (WH)

Two of Spetchley's pretty cottages, *c.* 1906. Above, Marl Bank Cottage; below, the Old Rectory. (WH)

Norton and Kempsey

Norton is a small village mainly renowned for being the former home of the Worcestershire Regiment. Just outside the village, the main Birmingham to Bristol railway line is joined by the Worcester line: it is here that many would like to see the construction of a parkway station that would enable Worcester to take a greater part in the inter-city network. Perhaps fortunately for the villagers this still appears to be a somewhat forlorn hope. Kempsey grew up on the old coaching road out of Worcester and until the construction of the M5 motorway had to bear more than its fair share of passing traffic. The main road through Kempsey is full of interest, as Georgian and Victorian houses mingle with local shops and drinking houses. Off the main road, however, estates of varied newer housing give Kempsey the inevitable dormitory status of a village that lies close to the city.

Norton School, *c.* 1905. This building has now been converted into a private residence.

Norton Barracks, *c.* 1910. Now deserted, it awaits an uncertain fate.

Norton Barracks staged the army rugby semi-final in October 1913.

Norton Junction station, *c*. 1907. This station was closed several years ago.

Church Street, Kempsey, *c.* 1908. Edwin Wintle's carpentry premises are on the right. Church Street has also been known locally as Pig Lane. (WH)

The Auborne Tree, Church Street, *c.* 1935. The tree was destroyed by a storm in 1974 and was also known as the Albion Tree. On the right is a timbered almshouse and the Dame's School.

Kempsey church, *c.* 1910. The church of St Mary was consecrated by Bishop Giffard in 1288. (PP)

The Original Stores, Kempsey, *c.* 1938. Horace Quarmby was the shopkeeper and his delivery bicycle stands outside.

Deep snow in Kempsey, *c.* 1917. On the right is the Talbot Hotel, then run by Harry Hopkins. (MX)

all are photo

This fine Georgian house in Kempsey was a private hotel in 1929.

Kempsey Common, *c.* 1936. During the Second World War part of this common was ploughed up and cultivated in order to provide extra food.

Flooded meadows at Kempsey in August 1912. I wonder if they talked of water shortages in those days! (MX)

Kerswell Green, *c.* 1910. (PP)

Pixham Ferry, *c.* 1910. This was a large ferry vehicle and it moved across the Severn by means of a submerged chain. There was no road across Kempsey Ham to gain access to the ferry so the journey was somewhat hazardous! Frequent users of the ferry were the local foxhounds. The ferry virtually ceased operation in 1939. By crossing the river at this point we reach our next destination – Callow End.

SECTION FIVE

Callow End and Powick

These are two very pleasant villages, although the presence of the main Worcester to Malvern road undoubtedly diminishes the charm of Powick. Callow End is fortunate in lying on a quieter road and is overlooked by the convent of Stanbrook Abbey. The majority of the superb photographs in this section were once the property of Miss Mollie Smith. Mollie evidently worked at Beauchamp Court in some capacity during the early years of this century, while her mother probably lived at Little Otherton, near Cotheridge. Mollie was a teenager with a great love of life and she socialized with many friends of both sexes. She also appears to have had an ardent interest in the theatre. One of Mollie's admirers sent her a 'Certificate of Proficiency in the Art of Spooning'. This proclaimed 'that the pretty and winsome Miss Smith having passed the final examination before the National Matchmaking Association, and taken her diploma (she being over sixteen) is now fully qualified for commencing the gentle art of Flirtation. A word to the wise is sufficient. Applicants will kindly call round at the back door after seven any evening and will please bring meat to quieten the bulldog.'

The Ferry House, Callow End, *c.* 1912. The writer informs us that this was also a farm where milk and cream could be obtained.

The new clubroom at Callow End, *c.* 1908.

Callow End in the 1920s. The Old Bush Inn is hidden behind the house in the middle background.

The Blue Bell at Callow End, devastated by fire, *c.* 1909. Licensee George Wallace sent his children (Ethel and Winifred) to stay with the village policeman (Mr Beswick) until the Blue Bell was habitable again.

Local men outside the Blue Bell, *c.* 1910.

Beauchamp Court, Callow End, *c.* 1907. This was where Mollie Smith worked for William Henry Gabb – a farmer and hop grower.

The Old Hills, Callow End, *c.* 1906. This is a popular area for walking, affording fine views of the Malvern Hills.

William Henry Stephens Brickell was the proprietor of the Callow End bakery, which still operates today.

Two fine farming scenes from the Mollie Smith collection. I wonder if Mollie appears in the photograph below? (AC)

Kents Green Court Lodge, Callow End, *c.* 1925.

Powick police station, *c.* 1908. The policeman posing for the camera is thought to be Henry Young. This building may still be seen on the Powick to Callow End road.

Mollie received this humorous card from her friend Alice in October 1906. Alice writes: 'I had a most ripping time at Colwall, also yesterday what grand weather. . . .'

Powick Asylum, *c.* 1907.

SECTION SIX

Leigh, Leigh Sinton, Alfrick and Suckley

Set amid glorious Worcestershire countryside that is well worthy of further exploration, these villages retain much of their original character. Hop growing was of prime importance in the first half of this century and in the summer the countryside was invaded by pickers from the towns of Worcestershire and the Black Country. Many of these travelled by train and would alight at Leigh Court or Suckley station. From the station they were picked up by farm wagons and transported to the various hopyards. These people were rough and ready and their manners and language no doubt left a lot to be desired! But this was an escape from the drab lives they led in the smokey towns and both farmer and picker gained financially from the arrangement. The seasonal invaders and the railway are now but memories.

Leigh Court Farm and church, *c.* 1940. Leigh Court Farm is the location of the oldest fully cruck-built barn in Great Britain. It was built by the abbots of Pershore in the early fifteenth century.

Brace's, near Leigh Sinton, *c.* 1910. I am told that this house had a majestic Jacobean staircase, but unfortunately it was demolished in recent times. (HI)

Hayley Dingle, between Leigh and Alfrick, *c.* 1920. The railway bridge was part of the Worcester to Bromyard branch line. The remaining parts of this bridge are now largely obscured by trees and undergrowth. (PP)

Brooklands, Leigh, *c.* 1920. (PP)

Leigh Sinton, *c.* 1920. (PP)

Hop workers in the fields of James and William H. Leeke, Great House Farm, Leigh. (AC)

A rare interior view of the hopworks at J. and W.H. Leeke. (PP)

Hop workers proudly display their pickings. Note the poor chap using a hook to support the sack. (PP)

Done's Cottage, Alfrick, *c.* 1904.

Cherry Green, Alfrick, *c.* 1907. This was a nursery ran by Albert Warskitt and was well known for its growing of narcissi.

The blacksmiths shop, Alfrick, *c.* 1910. The cart belongs to E.J. Spencer – the local butcher.

The Meet at Alfrick Pound. Alfrick bakery is on the right.

The Chantry, Suckley, *c.* 1906. In residence at this time were the Addis sisters.

A thatcher at work in the Suckley area, *c.* 1912.

SECTION SEVEN

Broadwas and Knightwick

Broadwas is a quiet, picturesque village set amid rich meadows and uplands and located on the north bank of the River Teme. At one time it was famous for its cider, which was a favourite tipple of the hop pickers. Knightwick lies just beyond Broadwas and was a prime hop growing area. Knightwick station was heavily used by the visiting hop pickers. Hops are still grown in this area today, but lack the importance they once had. Knightwick has always been a popular tourist spot and many of the postcards I possess of this place were sent by holiday-makers to their envious friends and relatives back home. The Talbot Hotel and smaller hostelries catered well for the visitor whether on foot, bicycle or four wheels. Fishermen, too, were attracted to the area by the plentiful grayling and chub of the Teme. Ankerdine Hill, just to the north of Knightwick, affords glorious views of the surrounding countryside and was often visited by Queen Adelaide when she was in residence at Witley Court in the 1840s.

Broadwas, *c.* 1935.

A fine study of locals outside the butchers shop of William Spencer, Broadwas, *c.* 1908.

The blacksmiths shop at Broadwas, *c.* 1908. This was run by James Hill, who was also the sub-postmaster.

The maypole at Broadwas School, *c.* 1908.

The Cedars, Broadwas, *c.* 1906. (WH)

Broadwas Court, *c.* 1916. (WH)

The Worcestershire Hounds meet outside the Talbot Hotel, Knightwick, *c.* 1909.

An unidentified gathering outside the Talbot Hotel. (AC)

Two views of the Ankerdine Tea Rooms.

The Grange, Knightwick, *c.* 1908. Mrs Cranke offered 'superior apartments in a beautiful situation, punt on river for fishing, and good stabling'.

The Laurels at Ankerdine served teas to trippers in the 1920s.

Knightwick Sanatorium in the 1920s.

A patient smiles for the camera in January 1926. (WW)

SECTION EIGHT

Martley and Wichenford

Martley has been a large village within an extensive parish for many years, and even possessed a forbidding union workhouse which as late as 1924 housed ninety inmates. Situated on a secondary road, Martley retains much of its original charm and possesses many interesting buildings. Most notable of these is probably The Noak, which for many years was the home of the Nash family (to which belonged the Revd Treadway Russell Nash of Bevere – the distinguished local historian). Martley remains an important village as the Chantry School and local industrial estate indicate. Wichenford is a fairly secluded agricultural village served only by minor roads and farmsteads and cottages are scattered over a wide area. In the church are monuments to the Washbournes – an ancient family whose residence was Wichenford Court. The only public house is the Masons Arms situated at Castle Hill and some distance from the heart of the village.

Martley, *c.* 1908.

The Crown Hotel, Martley, *c.* 1905. Edward Lawson was the licensee. In the middle background is the future site of the post office.

The post office, Martley, photographed shortly after it was built.

Martley church undergoing repair. The church was reopened in December 1909. (AC)

The Scar Bank, Martley, c. 1908.

The Stores, Martley, c. 1940. Mrs Mary Fidoe was the proprietress.

Wichenford Court, *c.* 1908. This is now the
home of Colonel and Mrs Patrick Britten.
(WH)

An ancient barn in the grounds of Wichenford Court, *c.* 1931. (WC)

The dovecote at Wichenford Court, *c.* 1908. (WH)

The Shelsleys and Clifton-on-Teme

These villages remain comparatively remote from Worcester and seem to have changed little over the years. This is an area of glorious rolling countryside with fertile soil that continues to support many scattered farms. Here the Teme Valley, with its steep sides and dingle valleys, woodlands and fast-flowing rivers and streams, gives this high part of Worcestershire a charm all of its own. Clifton was once a market town, being given borough status by Henry III in 1270. This gave it the right to hold markets and fairs, but like many other medieval townships Clifton is now no more than a picturesque village.

All Saints church, Shelsley Beauchamp. (HB)

Shelsley Beauchamp School and pupils, *c*. 1906.

Brockhill Hotel, near Shelsley Beauchamp. (HB)

A general view of Shelsley Beauchamp, *c.* 1908.

Shelsley Grange, *c*. 1904. The owner then was Lady Hughes. (AC)

A typical hopfield scene, *c*. 1910. (AC)

Hop drying at Shelsley Walsh, *c*. 1906. (WH)

Jack Woodhouse on his Ivy-Precision at Shelsley Walsh. This advertisement card proclaimed the excellence of Vacuum Mobiloil B.

New Mill Bridge, Shelsley. The cows show their usual interest in the photographer!

Clifton, *c.* 1905. This view, with the Red Lion public house on the left, is little changed today.

Clifton Memorial Hall, *c.* 1925. This was opened in 1922.

The bus driver seems keen to pose for the camera in this view of Clifton, *c.* 1938. (WC)

CNNE.1F.   MAIN STREET. CLIFTON UPON TEME.

A more recent view of Clifton, featuring the well-known Yeomans Garage.

Great Witley

Great Witley is inevitably dominated by the brooding presence of Witley Court despite its present condition. The court was severely ravaged by fire in 1937 and for nearly thirty years the elements, neglect and vandalism contributed to its further downfall. Fortunately English Heritage is now custodian of the court and the ruins are being painstakingly restored. The Foley family, who had made their fortune from iron, were not only responsible for the rise of Witley Court but also for the present position of the village of Great Witley. The Foleys did not want their views spoilt by the houses of the villagers so they persuaded them to move up the road! The present-day village remains largely unspoilt and possesses varied buildings of considerable style and charm. The Hundred House is pre-eminent and was built in the eighteenth century by Lord Foley. This replaced an earlier inn in order to provide superior accommodation for visiting gentry.

Witley Court, *c.* 1908. Thanks to the sterling efforts of the Poseidon Fountain Restoration Society it is possible that one day the fountain on the right will again become fully operational.

Witley Court viewed from the east, *c*. 1930.

An unusual view of the Orangery in all its glory.

The magnificent and immaculate gardens, *c*. 1908.

The Hundred House in the 1930s. I can personally recommend this as a place to hold your wedding reception!

The doctor's house in the early 1900s.

'Anyone for tennis' at the White House, *c.* 1910. This large house has been split into two dwellings.

Great Witley School, *c.* 1908, complete with happy pupils.

The Worcester road, looking towards the Hundred House, in the 1930s.

Ramblers near Great Witley.

SECTION ELEVEN

Ombersley and Around

Ombersley is an ancient and pretty village within an extensive parish that contains several small hamlets and villages. Ombersley Court is the home of the Sandys family and lies hidden away from public gaze to the west of the village centre. By walking through the tranquil surroundings of the village churchyard you may catch a glimpse of the impressive court and its wooded grounds. Ombersley is well known for its picturesque black and white cottages, which have appeared on countless postcards over the years. Therefore I have concentrated mainly on illustrating other aspects of the parish, including some of the fine public houses in the area.

The Cross, Ombersley in the 1920s. This postcard was published for J. Morris – a local shopkeeper.

Ombersley, looking towards Worcester, *c.* 1935. Is the lone cyclist slowing down for the camera?

The Crown Hotel, Ombersley, *c.* 1925. Now known as the Crown and Sandys Arms, this is an atmospheric place to wine and dine.

Two fine examples of thatched cottages at Uphampton, *c.* 1925. This hamlet now boasts seventeen Grade II listed buildings, one of the highest concentrations in the area.

The Oldfield Inn, near Ombersley, with a view towards Kidderminster, *c.* 1923. The licensee, Richard Brooks, previously had been a market gardener.

The Mitre Oak at Crossway Green, *c.* 1910. A much larger hotel now stands on this spot.

An early local motor omnibus on the route between Worcester, Ombersley and Holt Fleet, *c.* 1912. This vehicle (registration no. U771) was probably the first Brush vehicle ever produced.

Hadley Bowling Green Inn, *c.* 1910. This inn has recently undergone extensive refurbishment. (WH)

The Dorothy Café, Holt Fleet, c. 1935. This is now a small supermarket.

Holt Castle, Holt Heath, c. 1938, supposedly built by the D'Abitots during the Norman period. The more modern portion was restored in 1868.

Sinton Green, Monkwood Green and Hallow

Sinton Green is a very pleasant village with a large green. The pond on the green silted up about fifty years ago, but has recently been recreated by local volunteers. Nearby is the Monkwood Nature Reserve, noted for its numerous butterflies. Monkwood Green is a quiet place dotted with varied dwellings. Social activity centres on the Fox, where the cider is heartily recommended. Hallow is a large village that sprawls along the Worcester to Tenbury road. While the village green remains picturesque, a fair number of quaint thatched cottages have disappeared over the years. These have been replaced by more nondescript buildings, so Hallow lacks some of the charm it formerly had. Although it must be considered a dormitory village there is still a strong sense of community, as made clear by the activities of the local church, the Hallow Horticultural Society, the Women's Institute and various sporting clubs.

Sinton Green, *c.* 1910. This shows the original pond.

The Live and Let Live, Oakhall Green, *c.* 1908. The licensee was then a Mr S. Mann. This public house is now known as The Hunters Lodge.

The New Inn, Sinton Green, *c.* 1910. John Evans was the licensee.

The Fox at Monkwood Green, *c.* 1930. Emily Allen was the landlady.

The Fox pictured only a few years later. Horace Winders is supporting the wall! (WC)

Hallow, *c.* 1920, looking northwards from the village green. (PP)

Young girls galore at Hallow Green on the occasion of the local Meet of the foxhounds, *c.* 1910.

Hallow Green, *c.* 1910, looking up Church Lane. At the end of the lane is the site of the old church, which was destroyed in 1830 and replaced by an aisleless building. This was in turn pulled down when the present structure was erected in 1868. The old graveyard still remains and contains the grave of Sir Charles Bell (discoverer of the distinct functions of the nerves), who died at Hallow Park in 1842.

Hallow Post Office, *c.* 1930. Only the building on the far right now survives.

The butchers shop, Hallow, in September 1919.

The Royal Oak, Hallow, *c.* 1908. Henry Pratt was the landlord and the baby in arms is Vin Pratt – his son.

The Ancient Order of Foresters (4964 Lodge) gathered outside The Crown Inn, Hal
in June 1909, on the occasion of the annual fête. Henry Lock was the landlord, ar

ight to be the chap in the light jacket and bowler hat standing to the left of the bands-
. (WTC)

Camp Lock in the 1920s. (PP)

Looking towards Hallow from the Camp in the 1920s. The Camp Inn is obscured by trees. (PP)

Broadheath, Kenswick and Crown East

Broadheath is a sprawling village divided by its large common, where Sir Edward Elgar loved to walk. The heart of the village centres on Lower Broadheath, where small estates of new housing are largely inhabited by the commuting classes. Broadheath also possesses three public houses of character – the Bell Inn, the Dew Drop Inn and the Plough Inn. There is no village at Kenswick and the population of this parish in 1901 was a mere thirty-five. Most of these people would have been associated, no doubt, with Kenswick Manor and its farming. Crown East is a small linear hamlet, with a small and beautiful church. Farming and market gardening are still of some importance in this area.

The approach to Lower Broadheath from Worcester, *c.* 1924. (PP)

Two views of the Martley Road in Lower Broadheath, *c.* 1910.

Martley Road, Lower Broadheath, *c.* 1920. The cart in the background is that of J. Hope – the local decorator. (PP)

Broadheath Memorial Hall was erected in memory of Admiral Britten (d. 1910) by the Honourable Mrs Britten. This is believed to be the opening ceremony. The delightful hall has now been ruined visually by a modern extension.

Broadheath Scout troop, *c*. 1912. Back row, left to right: Forrester Britten, Neil Wier (Scoutmaster), the Reverend Mr Griffiths, Charles Britten. On the front row, the Scout fifth from the left is Harold Boulton.

Broadheath School on Empire Day, *c.* 1912.

Two views of lovely cottages that used to exist in the vicinity of Jacomb Road, Lower Broadheath. In the photograph below, Jim Griffiths sits on his hobby horse.

Sir Edward Elgar was born at this pretty cottage in Upper Broadheath in June 1857. This is a marvellous place to visit, with glorious views towards the Malvern Hills. (GH)

The Apostles was one of Elgar's three great oratorios.

Kenswick Manor was for many years the home of the Britten family. The postcard above was sent to Lieutenant-Colonel F.C.R. Britten when he was serving in Freiburg, Germany. Kenswick Manor is now a nursing home.

Patrick Britten celebrated his coming of age on 29 January 1938. These photographs were taken at Kenswick Manor.

Crown East, showing the church and the school, *c*. 1910.

Crown East, looking towards Lower Broadheath, *c*. 1930. This postcard was another in the series published for J.H. Chalke at the Rushwick Post Office.

SECTION FOURTEEN

Stockton and Abberley

Stockton is situated about fourteen miles out of Worcester, on the road to Tenbury Wells. It is only a small hamlet but has old buildings well worthy of inspection. Abberley is a large loose-knit village which lies amid lovely wooded hills and sprawls out over the common. Abberley Hall, built by the Moilliets in the middle of the nineteenth century, is now a school. It possesses a lofty detached clock tower which commands the beautiful valley of the Teme and looks down haughtily on the sad ruins of Witley Court. Despite the closeness of Abberley to Great Witley they remain distinct entities.

The blacksmith's shop, Stockton, *c.* 1910. Among those pictured is Anthony Field and his daughter Lotty. (AC)

Stockton Court, *c*. 1912.

The Rectory, Stockton, *c*. 1926.

This lady is well dressed for Stockton's annual fête. (AC)

The Stores, Abberley, *c*. 1925.

Abberley Common, *c*. 1930.

Apostles Oak, Abberley, *c.* 1912. This was named after an oak tree that stood near the lodge of Abberley Hall until it was burnt down in 1753. Tradition identifies this as Augustine's Oak, where St Augustine met the bishops of the Britons in AD 603. However, at least five other places also claim to have been the scene of this meeting!

A more recent view of Abberley, looking towards Abberley Hill.

CORONATION BONFIRE ON THE HILL ABBERLEY

A large coronation bonfire at Abberley – probably built for the accession of King George V.

Postcard Mysteries

Perhaps you would like to help me solve some of the mysteries I have in my collection! The following postcards are all of local origin but cannot be identified or categorized in any other way. No prizes are offered, but I hope you will have fun racking your brains and scratching your heads! If nothing else, this will serve as a reminder to record all relevant information on your own precious photographs and postcards.

A gathering near the village church. But who are they and where? (MF)

A collapsed building near a steep slope – possibly a railway embankment. Note the boy's blurred face on the left. What was this building and why did it collapse? (MF)

This horse and carriage is parked outside a local hostelry. The licensee is probably a Mr Potter ('otter' is discernible on the sign) which could make this The Gun Tavern, Newtown Road, Worcester. Can anyone confirm or dispute this?

An unidentified impressive house. The writer describes it as the 'Old Shanty'. So where is this building and does it exist today? (AC)

This postcard was purchased from a dealer in New Zealand and was photographed by H.A. Stretton of No. 302 Ombersley Road, Worcester, around 1917. Does anyone recognize these people – who were probably related to a Frederick H. Howell?

A mean looking football team poses for the camera, c. 1910. Does anyone recognize the venue or the team? (HI)